MIND MAGIC
GUIDED IMAGERY
WORKBOOK

Stacking My Blocks for
Emotional Well-Being

Janice McDermott, M.Ed, MSW

BALBOA.PRESS

A DIVISION OF HAY HOUSE

Balboa Press books may be ordered through booksellers or by contacting:

Balboa Press
A Division of Hay House
1663 Liberty Drive
Bloomington, IN 47403
www.balboapress.com
844-682-1282

Because of the dynamic nature of the Internet, any web addresses or links contained in this book may have changed since publication and may no longer be valid. The views expressed in this work are solely those of the author and do not necessarily reflect the views of the publisher, and the publisher hereby disclaims any responsibility for them.

The author of this book does not dispense medical advice or prescribe the use of any technique as a form of treatment for physical, emotional, or medical problems without the advice of a physician, either directly or indirectly. The intent of the author is only to offer information of a general nature to help you in your quest for emotional and spiritual well-being. In the event you use any of the information in this book for yourself, which is your constitutional right, the author and the publisher assume no responsibility for your actions.

Any people depicted in stock imagery provided by Getty Images are models, and such images are being used for illustrative purposes only.
Certain stock imagery © Getty Images.

Print information available on the last page.

ISBN: 978-1-9822-7242-5 (sc)
ISBN: 978-1-9822-7243-2 (e)

Balboa Press rev. date: 08/02/2021

CONTENTS

KINDS OF GUIDED IMAGERY

1. **Feeling State Imagery:** Change mood. Any imagery that can elicit a delightful feeling and replace doubt, fear or anxiety.

2. **End State Imagery:** Uses for its content any desired outcome or goal.

3. **Energetic Imagery:** Any image that generates an internal feeling of motion or the movement of time.

4. **Cellular Imagery:** Uses accurate medical information but focuses on the healthy interaction of cells.

5. **Physiological Imagery:** Similar to Cellular imagery only larger in scope, imagining the shrinking of a tumor.

6. **Psychological Imagery:** Built around real-life issues, such as walking through your recently burnt home to cope with the loss.

7. **Metaphoric Imagery:** Uses symbols in place of reality, such as the planting of a seed as a symbol of dying.

8. **Spiritual Imagery:** includes religious or spiritual references such as hearing the voice of God in the wind, creates a sense of oneness, transcendence.

But words are things, and a small drop of ink, falling like dew, upon a thought, produces that which makes thousands, perhaps millions, think.   —Lord Byron

COMMUNICATION PROCESS DIAGRAM

(INPUT)

1. External Events: Sensory input –V, A, K, O, G

(ENCODE)

2. Internal Processing Filters: Determines how information is deleted or distorted for generalizing

    A. Meta Programs

        1) Internal process

        2) Internal state

    B. Attitudes: Values and Beliefs

    C. Memories:

        1) Representation of time

        2) Conscious/unconscious decisions

(DELETE)

3. Universal Modeling Process: The mind only holds between 5-7 items of information, at one time. We choose one sense out of five–V, A, K, O, G for foreground as in *Comparative Deletion, Unspecified Verb, Nominalization,* and *Lack of Referential Index.*

(DISTORT):

4. Misrepresenting Reality (aids in motivation)

    A. Mind Reading

    B. Lost Performatives

    C. Complex Equivalence

    D. Cause-Effect

(GENERALIZE):

5. Internal Representation

    A. Universal Qualifier

    B. Modal Operators

(DECODE)

6. Internal Representation: Internal Images

(OUTPUT)

7. Language Representation: Words representing the images

> *Healing Mind, Five Steps to Ultimate Healing, Four Rooms for Thoughts: Achieve Satisfaction through a Well-Managed Mind*
>
> —Janice. McDermott, M Ed., MSW

LESSON I: MANAGING MY BODY

Answer on day five of daily imagery

1. **My hardest to relax muscle group is my**

2. **When I relax all my muscles, I feel**

3. **I get more tense when**

4. **Other than sleeping, I am the most relaxed when I**

On the image below highlight, the area where you are the most tense—most of the time.

LESSON 2: LEARNING TO BREATHE

Complete on Day 5

1. **Describe your experience**

   Intake:

2. **Pause between intake and release. Describe how your body feels?**

3. **Release/out breath. Describe how this feels different from your in-breath.**

4. **List situations when focusing on breathing to calm yourself can be useful.**

LESSON 3: FOREGROUND AND BACKGROUND

Figure A (artist unknown)

Which is foreground for you, black or white? We each have a preference as to which we see first.

Figure B (artist unknown)

Is your foreground/background preference still the same when viewing Figure B?

By being able to shift between foreground and background we grow in understanding of another's point of view and in that way, we become more forgiving and compassionate.

LESSON 4: SEEING WHAT I SEE

DAY I:

Draw or write a description of your experience

DAY 2:

Draw or write a description of your experience

DAY 3:

Draw or write a description of your experience

DAY 4:

Draw or write a description of your experience

DAY 5:

Draw or explain how using your imagination can be useful in creating your future.

LESSON 5: HEARING WHAT I HEAR

DAY 1:

Draw or write a description of your experience.

DAY 2:

Draw or write a description of your experience.

DAY 3:

Draw or write a description of your experience.

DAY 4:

Draw or write a description of your experience.

DAY 5:

Draw or write a description of your experience.

LESSON 6: FEELING THE WORLD AROUND ME

DAY 1:

Draw or write a description of your experience.

DAY 2:

Draw or write a description of your experience.

DAY 3:

Draw or write a description of your experience.

DAY 4:

Draw or write a description of your experience.

DAY 5:

Draw or write a description of your experience.

LESSON 7: SMELLING AND TASTING

DAY I:

Draw or write a description of your experience.

DAY 2:

Draw or write a description of your experience

DAY 3:

Draw or write a description of your experience.

DAY 4:

Draw or write a description of your experience.

DAY 5:

Draw or write a description of your experience.

LESSON 8: FEELING SAFE

DAY I:

Write about or draw your safe place.

DAY 2: What sounds help you feel safe?

DAY 3: What body sensations feel like safe signals?

DAY 4: Describe other things including taste that add to your feeling safe.

DAY 5: Who are the top two people to whom you might tell about your safe space?

LESSON 9: SHIFTING PERCEPTION SHIFTING EMOTIONS

Circle the one that applies.

DAY 1: VISUAL:

1. My feeling gets stronger when what I am thinking about is in

    a) color

    b) black and white

2. My feeling gets stronger when what I am thinking is

    a) near

    b) far away

3. My feeling gets stronger when what I am thinking is

    a) moving

    b) still

4. My feeling gets stronger when I am

    a) in the picture

    b) out of the picture watching what I am thinking

Circle the one that applies.

DAY 2: AUDITORY:

My mad feeling becomes less when I change the

a) volume,   **b) speed,**   or   **c) rhythm**

of what I am thinking.

DAY 3: KINESTHETIC:

1. My Sad feeling becomes less when what I am thinking is in

   a) color   **b) black and white.**

2. My Sad feeling becomes less when what I am thinking is

   a) near   **b) far away.**

3. My Sad feeling becomes less when what I am thinking is

   a) moving   **b) still.**

4. My Sad feeling becomes less when I am

   a) in the picture   **b) out of the picture**

of what I am thinking.

LESSON 10: ANCHORING WITH TRANSITIONAL OBJECTS

DAY I: What object did you select as your talisman?

DAY 2: Did you remember to take your object inward?

DAY 3: Name some *visual* characteristics of your success.

DAY 4: Name some *auditory* characteristics of your success.

DAY 5: List your body *sensations* that help you imagine success.

LESSON 11: EXPLORING MY WORLD

DAY I:

Write about or draw your experience.

DAY 2:

Write about or draw your experience.

DAY 3:

Write about or draw your experience.

DAY 4:

Write or draw about your experience.

DAY 5:

Write about or draw your safe place.

LESSON 12: MENDING WHAT'S BROKEN

IMAGE COMPONENT COMPARISON LIST

DAY: 1

Write your limiting success sentence.

Circle all that match your limiting vision.

LIMITING
COLOR
BLACK & WHITE
NEAR
FAR
MOVING
STILL
YOU ARE IN IT
YOU ARE OUT OF IT

DAY: 2

Circle all that make no change to your limiting sentence.

NO DIFFERENCE
COLOR
BLACK & WHITE
NEAR
FAR
MOVING
STILL
YOU ARE IN IT
YOU ARE OUT OF IT

DAY: 3

Circle all that make your limiting sentence no longer limiting. Repeat as many times as needed to imagine success.

ENHANCING
COLOR
BLACK & WHITE
NEAR
FAR
MOVING
STILL
YOU ARE IN IT
YOU ARE OUT OF IT

DAY: 4

1. **Write your success enhancing sentence.**

2. **List one or two components of your success enhancing statement that are different from your limiting statement.**

DAY: 5

Use colored pencils, markers or even fabrics to illustrate your feeling of success.

LESSON 13: THE HOUSE OF MIND

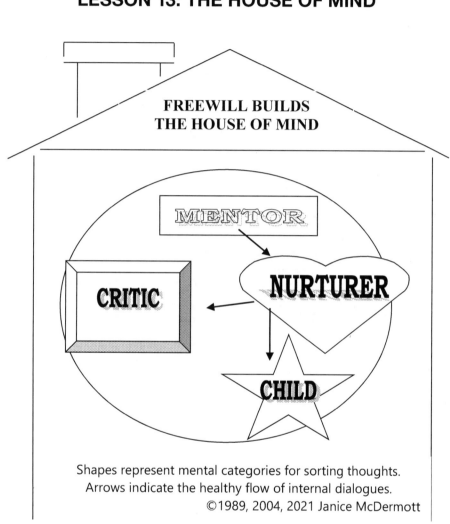

FREEWILL BUILDS
THE HOUSE OF MIND

MENTOR

CRITIC

NURTURER

CHILD

Shapes represent mental categories for sorting thoughts.
Arrows indicate the healthy flow of internal dialogues.
©1989, 2004, 2021 Janice McDermott

ROOMS OF THE MIND CHARACTERISTICS

Mentor (Rectangle)

1. Stores time, sequence of events, and other information as a computer would (think of a robot)

2. Non-emotional

3. Contains factual data

4. Contains accumulated beliefs and Values, (even when contradictory)

5. Knows the positive intent of other dialogues

6. Constructive

Critic (Square)

1. Incapable of love

2. Guiltless

3. Can appear suddenly

4. Attempts to gain recognition, remain important

5. Eavesdrops and interrupts other mental processes

6. Creates personal suffering, illusion of separateness and despair, and is destructive

Nurturer (Heart)

1. Buffers the effects of the Critic

2. Unconditionally loving even to the Critic

3. Peaceful, forgiving

4. Non-judgmental, accepting, validating

5. intuitive, creative

6. Protective, instructive

7. Purposeful

Child (Star)

1. Ceaselessly creative

2. Finds a sense of value present in everything

3. Spontaneous

4. Source of all basic emotions

5. Eternally connected to the non-physical

OBSERVING MY MIND QUESTIONNAIRE

Answer the following questions for each day.

Day 1: The Mentor

Write about how you can tell when you are in your

Mentor Mind:

Mentor Body:

Day 2: The Critic

1. Write a sentence you hear in the room of the Critic.

2. Is it male or female?

3. Describe what happens to your body when you listen to this critical voice?

4. Name the two significant people whose voices or images live through you in the room of your mind called the *Critic*.

5. Who talks the most or has the loudest voice?

6. What is their favorite thing to say to you that makes you feel smaller, weaker or dumber?

Day 3: The Nurturer

1. Write the words you hear in the room of the *Nurturer*.

2. Is the voice Male or Female?

3. Name two significant people whose voices live through their voices in the room of your mind labeled *Nurturer*.

4. Which one has the most comforting voice or expression?

5. What happens in your body when you listen to this voice?

6. What is your favorite thing said in this room that makes you feel bigger stronger, more confident?

Day 4: The Child

Circle what is needed by the child in your room of *Child*.

Love

Understanding

Actively engaged

Positive attention

Security

Companionship

Information

Freedom of imagination

Day 5: My House of Mind

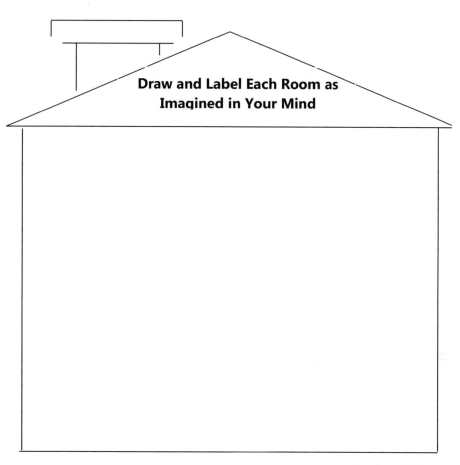

Draw and Label Each Room as
Imagined in Your Mind

LESSON 14: ACCEPTING MY SELVES

DAY 1: Write a description of your

    1. Chosen self

    2. Shadow self

DAY 2: Take Another Look from a Different Point of View

Write a new description of your

1. **Chosen Self**

2. **Shadow Self**

DAY 3: Use color, sound, sensations, taste and smell in your written description.

My balloon is

Our mixed balloon is

DAY 5

1. Make a list of words to describe your animal

2. Draw an outline picture of your animal

LESSON 15: PRAISING SELF AND OTHERS

DAY I: Praising My self

1. Write your praise sentence.

2. In addition to yourself, identify someone who also deserves to hear your praise sentence.

DAY 2: More Praise

1. Write a new praise sentence.

2. In addition to yourself, identify someone who also deserves to hear your praise sentence.

DAY 3: More Praise

1. Write a third praise sentence.

2. In addition to yourself, identify someone who also deserves to hear your praise sentence.

DAY 4: More Praise

1. Write a fourth praise sentence.

2. In addition to yourself, identify someone else who also deserves to hear your praise sentence.

LESSON 16: WINDS OF CHANGE

DAY 1:

1. Write about or draw one of your *harmful* behaviors.

2. Describe how you feel (mad, glad, sad, or afraid) about this behavior.

DAY 2:

1. Write about or draw another one of your *harmful* behaviors.

2. Describe how you feel about this behavior.

DAY 3:

1. Write about or draw one of your *helpful* behaviors.

2.   Describe how you feel about this behavior.

DAY 4:

1. Write about or draw another one of your *helpful* behaviors.

2. Describe how you feel about this behavior

DAY 5:

1.   Write about or draw another one of your *helpful* behaviors.

2.   Describe how you feel about this behavior

Lesson 16: Your Contract for Change

(Independent Activity)

I _____, choose to release the
following behaviors that are harmful to me and to replace them with helpful behaviors
that will create the future I want.

I Release and Replace
My **Negative** Behaviors with My **Positive** Behaviors

(List)	(List)

LESSON 17: CREATING SUCCESS

Day 1: Write two goals you would like to reach over the next two weeks.

Goal I:

Goal 2

DAY 2: Steps to accomplishing first goal, and those who can help

Steps

Helpers

DAY3: Complete the following goal setting worksheet

GOAL SETTING WORKSHEET

What You Need to Set a Useful Goal:

> ➢ **Specific intention:** Describe what you want to accomplish with as much detail as possible-including the date by which you want to accomplish the goal. (Ex. "I want to improve my overall grade in Spanish from a B to an A in nine weeks.")

> ➢ **A Goal That is Challenging and Possible:** it is possible to bring a subject up one letter grade over nine weeks. it would be unrealistic to expect to do so in one week.

Activity:

1. Write your goal and the date for accomplishing it.

   I choose to (goal):

   By (date): _____

2. List the first three steps to accomplishing your goal:

   I will

   a)

   b)

3. Name the people who will help or encourage you to reach your goal:

4. Describe how you will feel when you reach your goal.

WHEN I REACH MY GOAL, I WILL FEEL

DAY4: Complete the goal setting worksheet

GOAL SETTING WORKSHEET

What is Needed to Set a Useful Goal:

➤ **Specific intention:** Describe what you want to accomplish with as much detail as possible-including the date by which you want to accomplish the goal. (Ex. "I want to improve my overall grade in Spanish from a B to an A in nine weeks.")

➤ **A Goal That is Challenging and Possible:** it is possible to bring a subject up one letter grade over nine weeks. it would be unrealistic to expect to do so in one week.

Activity:

5. Write your goal and the date for accomplishing it.

   I choose to (goal):

   By (date): _____

6. List the first three steps to accomplishing your goal:

   I will

   c)

   d)

7. Name the people who will help or encourage you to reach your goal:

8. Describe how you will feel when you reach your goal.

WHEN I REACH MY GOAL, I WILL FEEL

DAY5: Complete the goal setting worksheet

GOAL SETTING WORKSHEET

What You Need to Set a Useful Goal:

➢ **Specific intention:** Describe what you want to accomplish with as much detail as possible-including the date by which you want to accomplish the goal. (Ex. "I want to improve my overall grade in Spanish from a B to an A in nine weeks.")

➢ **A Goal That is Challenging and Possible:** it is possible to bring a subject up one letter grade over nine weeks. it would be unrealistic to expect to do so in one week.

Activity:

9. Write your goal and the date for accomplishing it.

   I choose to (goal):

   By (date): _____

10. List the first three steps to accomplishing your goal:

    I will

    e)

    f)

11. Name the people who will help or encourage you to reach your goal:

12. Describe how you will feel when you reach your goal.

WHEN I REACH MY GOAL, I WILL FEEL

LESSON 18: BRIDGES TO THE FUTURE

MY FUTURE LIFE

DAY 1: Describe your life 10 years from now (Date: __/__/__):

A. Home:

B. Relationships (people or pets):

C. Type(s) of transportation:

D. Activities:

School

People

Work

Play

E. Other observations:

DAY 2: Describe your life 20 years from now (Date: __/__/__):

A. Home:

B. Relationships (people or pets):

C. Type(s) of transportation:

D. Activities:

School

People

Work

Play

E. Other observations:

About the Author

JANICE MCDERMOTT, M.ED, MSW—received both her Master's in Education and Master's in Social Work from Louisiana State University. Her Gestalt Diploma is from the Gestalt Institute of New Orleans with additional years of training at the Esalen Institute of California. She is a Licensed Clinical Social Worker and Clinical Diplomate, a School Social Work Specialist, and a certified Master Neurolinguistic Practitioner. Janice has been teaching patterns of communication since 1997. She authored, HEALING MIND, Five Steps to Ultimate Healing, Four Rooms for Thoughts: Achieve Satisfaction through a Well-Managed Mind, and MIND MAGIC, BUILDING A FOUNDATION FOR EMOTIONAL WELL-BEING.

Printed in the United States
by Baker & Taylor Publisher Services